Cunfushun
and **Calm**

Max proudly displaying his tattoos with his personal motto

Cunfushun
and Calm

Maximillian Miguel
Monroy-Miller

Poems | Photography | Drawings

MISSION POINT PRESS

Mission Point Press
2554 Chandler Road
Traverse City, Michigan 49696
www.MissionPointPress.com
231-421-9513

All photos by Max Monroy-Miller
with the exception of b&w family photos

Editor's note: The author took creative license with the
words in his poetry and other writings. Unusual spellings
and word usage were intentional.

Printed in the United States of America

ISBN: 978-1-950659-92-0
Library of Congress Control Number: (to come)

I got a lot of options
I don't know what 2 do
But if it were really up to me
I'd let it be up to you

Max Monroy-Miller

CONTENTS

3 WHISPER SCREAM
ADDICTION AND STRUGGLES

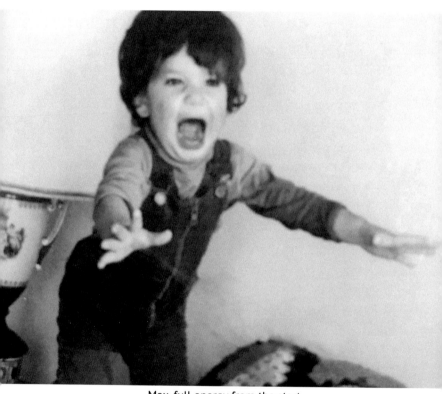
Max, full energy from the start.

JUST TELL THE STORY

I have a story to tell. It is the story of my son Max, my only child, a blessing to me and to many others. He was born in San Francisco in 1977 to me and his father Miguel Monroy. At that time, we considered ourselves a family with Ellin Woods and her son Ben, who was four months old when Max was born and continued to be his brother for the rest of Max's life. Max was a joy from the start, so easy to love. Happy, free-spirited and fearless. He loved his jolly jumper and his bottle. He loved to suck on a lemon. He loved to play. This family constellation lasted just a few years and then his father moved away and Ellin and Ben moved away. For the remainder of his childhood we were a family of two.

When Max was four years old, I made the difficult decision to move to rural Michigan to be close to our extended family. This meant Max would be distanced from his father and his California family for most of his childhood. Although I have some regrets for choosing this path, I believe the benefits outweighed the losses. Max attended Glen Lake Community school from kindergarten through high school. He was able to be a big fish in a small pond. He continued to be loved by all who helped to raise him. His grandma Jeannette had a special bond with Max as did his aunts Jannie, Nanny and Didi. His uncle Don stepped in and was a role model for Max. These years were mostly happy. He loved school and was successful academically, socially and athletically. In his senior year he was president of Student Council and a proud member of the 1994 State Championship

Football Team. He missed having his father around but he made the most of all he did have. We were blessed to have Tom, an exchange student from Germany, who became a brother for Max in all ways. After graduation he spent a year with Tom and his family in Germany where he enjoyed being part of a family with a father at the helm and siblings. He returned to attend Michigan State University in the fall of 1996.

He loved his college years where he found a missing connection to his Mexican American heritage. He found his brown and black brothers and founded a service fraternity called Omega Delta Phi. He was politically active and did well academically. He made lots of friends, male and female. He took advantage of many study-abroad experiences. He wrote poetry and performed spoken word. He became the best of himself. He shared his gifts readily.

By this time our free spirited wonderful young Max also learned to party hard. He learned to drink and smoke weed along with many others in college. He was the life of the party. Being so free and impulsive by nature there were times when he went too far. In 2001 he graduated from MSU and had to move on, saying good-by to his friends and the life he loved and the place where he felt so at home.

Max was accepted into Teach for America and was assigned to McAllen, Texas, a border town with a primarily Mexican population. He worked hard as a teacher and mentor to his students and had two very successful years. He continued to party hard for some relief from the demands of his work. Unfortunately, during this time he was introduced to cocaine. He struggled, mostly internally to find a way to manage his drug use but this drug proved to be too much for Max. He continued to do well in many aspects of his life, but as can be seen in his poems a battle was raging inside. Max's creative gifts flourished. He picked up a camera and took beautiful photos. He began to draw. He wrote poems from his heart. His internal struggles with addiction fueled his creativity. He traveled to Mexico and Europe seeking adventure and a broader experience of other cultures. It was during these years that he did much of his writings that are included in this collection.

Late in 2005 Max made the decision to return to Northern California hoping to reconnect with his father and his California family. He was very successful in finding a place to make a difference in the world by working in schools first as a middle school teacher and then as an administrator. He focused on a form of discipline called Restorative Practices in Oakland, California. He did an exemplary job and was able to influence many students. His big heart was full of compassion. He worked diligently to save his struggling students and provide opportunities for their success.

Sadly, his struggle with addiction progressed and began to take more of his life, eating away at his relationships and self-worth. Many who loved Max wanted to help him but the efforts of others could not make the necessary difference. This wonderful man that I was privileged to raise tried very hard to recover from his addiction. He made the kind of effort that he put out to save others. He was clean and sober for almost a year before returning to MSU in 2014 to study in a PHD program in Chicano Studies/Teacher Education. He brought his many gifts and his best efforts to these studies. He

Max with his Glen Lakers Varsity Teammates Tom and Todd

made new friends and did good work. His best efforts to change his life did not save him.

He died of a drug overdose during Spring Break 2016 while in the second year of his studies. He died of this terrible disease that continues to take the lives of too many wonderful people. Max left his family: his father Miguel, his sister Gabi, his grandmother Beatriz, and his many aunts, uncles and cousins, both Monroy and Miller who mourn his loss daily. He left many friends and colleagues who continue to hold him close in spirit. He left his beautiful fiancé, Heather, who he loved dearly, his ODPhi brothers, and all his hopes and dreams of creating a more just world. He left me, his Mom, who he wouldn't hurt for all the world. He left me to tell the story so that others might find understanding, recovery and hope. He left his poems and photos to share. He always told me that we must keep telling our stories. We must tell the true story. A happy, well loved, smart and talented man can become addicted and lose his life. That is the truth.

I hope that anyone who reads Max's poems will find insight and healing. The battle with addiction needs to be fought on many fronts; at our borders, in schools, and within families, through education, therapy and medical research, in 12 Step and other programs. Most importantly, the fight can only be won in the hearts and minds of those who suffer from this devastating disease.

Helping others was Max's passion. In sharing his story, I pray that someone who is suffering alone will reach out and find the love and support they need to recover. That would be the best legacy of Max.

Pat Miller, Max's mom

Max and Mom, Summer 2015.

Mommy and Max, calm.

WHERE ARE YOU?

Pat Miller

Four years and one month ago
you took your last breath
You died
Your body is gone
Your beautiful green eyes
Your perfect teeth
Your thick hair
Your smile

Where are you?
Your brain is quiet
No more thoughts
No more fears or worries
No more plans
No more problems to solve

Where are you?
No more fun adventures
No more hoops to shoot
Or movies to watch
Or fish to catch
No more hours on the pontoon late into the day
Or dips in the lake

Drawing of Mr. Love, Max Monroy-Miller

You are not here
Yet, you are not gone, not all the way
You are still around trying to reach me
Talk with me, to let me know something
Something important that you know
Now that your body and breathe are gone

Where are you now?
Your eyes live in your photos
Your heart is alive in your poems
The chime sounds in the wind
The red cardinal flies by
Your ashes rest peacefully under the willow
Four years and one month ago

You took your last breath
But you are still here
Your spirit lives and is near waiting for me to notice
Waiting for me to pay attention to this new way
we can be together

Max at the dunes, Glen Haven, Michigan

1

fREe-RUN

LOVE AND LIGHTER STUFF

Hanging off a cable car in San Francisco

WHO AM I

I am a lighter shade of brown
But I'm down
I'm a Xicano
People question me, they doubt me, they wonder
But I'm down
I love a warm tortilla con chorizo
And I love a thick hamburger with fries
But I'm down
I know every word to the latest rap tune and
I can barely dance the Quebradita
But I'm down
The whites say "What's all this Mexican stuff anyway?"
The Mexicans say "What's all these white ways,
can't you speak Spanish?"
But I'm down
People question my identity. They tell me who I am.
But I don't listen. I'm trapped between two walls
but I feel free.
I choose my identity and that is me.
I'm a lighter shade of brown, but don't ask me if I'm down.
Yo soy Xicano, pero mas important soy me.

MY ELDER

She was 90 years old
A walking museum
Her secrets whispered and told
I searched to free them
The memories
Nuggets of gold
Carrying a pass to my freedom

Max with his Abuela Beatriz Monroy.
Descansa en paz.

MY GRAMA

My Grama is Full Circle like Moon Cycle
She's a legendary earth Angel
We're Blessed 2 be with her now
As her loving spirit floats able
My Grama always matched her socks with her shirt
My Grama would meet me for lunch while I work
Then she'd eat a hot fudge sundae with whoever came in
And whoever else came in
And whoever else came in
My Grama had the Heart of a Lion
My Grama was defiant

And now my Grama is full circle like moon cycle
She's a Legendary Earth Angel
We're blessed to be with her now
As her loving spirit floats about

My Grama forgave to the grave
She can make each of your smile with one memory
She is the epitome of living pleasantly
She is Heavenly
My Grama's soul is captured in a Glen Lake Sunset
As it Ripples her goodbye wave
And by the way
My Grama rarely behaved
Thus, I'll never have to miss my Grama
Cuz my Grama will never go away
And she means that on this most wonderful day.
Cuz my Grama is Full Circle like moon cycle
She's a legendary Earth Angel
We're blessed to be with her now
As her loving spirit floats able

My Grama read me "Home for a Bunny," taught me cards,
And ate spoonsful of mayonnaise with me on the porch.
My Grama offered us so much
May we all carry her torch
My Grama is in all my love
She shares all my thoughts.
My Grama thinks every one of you are wonderful
She thinks all of your children are cute.
I Love Jeannette Miller
She's the path I knew
Blessed am I
The breath she blew
But we'll never have to miss Grama Miller
Cuz she'll never go away
You can see her in a Butterfly or a Trillium on a
Sunny Glen Lake Day.

Cuz my Grama is Full Circle like Moon Cycle
She's a legendary Earth Angel.
We're Blessed to be with her right now
As her loving spirit floats able.

Read at Jeannette Miller's Memorial
by Max. Old Settlers Picnic Grounds,
August 6, 2006

Max with dear family friend, Hannah, his 'sister from another mother'. Max wrote and delivered the following spoken word poem at Hannah's Bat Mitzvah.

HANNAH ROSSEN KOPEN *Cuz she's*
SHE RISES liKE SUNSHINE
B AND SHE'S FLOSSIN
LEAViN the Past ON A timeline
ON Route to the future
So chillax AND UNWIND
It's HARD to learn HEBREW
Now you A WOMAN — So cLEAR ya miND.

FAMily AND FRIENDS
TUNE iNTo Vocats I BlEND
HER StrENgth I cAN't COMpreheND
BABS + BAy — I got to commEND
INSpire yAll literally
SHE's the Nucleus or Epitome
Got plANS to sHARE My EpipHANY
A MirAcle PhysicAlly
~~CELEBRATE~~
YouR LiFE iS No MystERy
You DESTINED FoR History

BRilliANCE oF INNOCENCE
Logic iS NATurAl sENSE
No BouNDARIES
No DiFFIDENCE
IF GoD EXiSts
HANNAH'S Soul is the EviDENCE

WHAT MORE CAN I spit At y'all
54 AND she STANDIN tall
CAME out Fightin
No time to CRAWl
A Gift to us All
Piano AND BAll
YeH,
SHe iN FoR the long Haul.

CUZ SHE'S

HANNAH RossEN KopEN
SHe RiSeS liKE SuNsHiNE
13 AND SHE'S FlossiN
LEAViN the PAST oN A timelinE
ON Route to the Future
So CHillAX AND VNWIND
It's HARD to LEArN HebrEw
Now you A WoMAN - So CleAR YA MiND.

SHE'S Tops
LiKE BAgEls AND LoX
Love ContAgious liKE Pox
A HEART that won't stop
liKE the BEAT of Hip-Hop
SHe BRUsHED the DiRT oFF HeR SHouldE
Look AowFAST you got oLDER
NEVER GAVE VP liKE A soldieR
FRoM HANNUKAH to PAssoveR
Now its' timE to ConFEss
So
WE WiSH You the BEST

Yo
lessoNS gAiNED iN lifesTest
Flow
Tight with the Rest
~~tHE~~ WHOA!
YoU BoRN FREE
CHoosE to stay young.
~~tHE~~ ~~wAy~~ ~~yA~~ ~~huNG~~
BREAthE GiFtED
liVE By yA tongue
WARMth FElt
SHiNE liKE the SUN
CvZ yA RAyS BE thE GUN
SpRAy
AND WATCH yA DREAMS COmE
PAVE yA LegAcy HuN
WE loVE YOU A toN
AND THAT'S ONE.

CUZ SHES
HANNAH RossEN KopEN
SHE RiSeS liKE SuNSHiNE
13 AND S HE'S FlossiN
LEAViN the PAST oN A timeliNE
ON Route to the FUTURE
So CHillAX FN UNWIND
It HARD to lEArN HebrEw
Now you A WOMAN
So ClEAR YA MiND.

Time is Now
Pause Presence
Live For each Moment
Take Laughter + Clone it
An Angel
to Bless us
Your Future is Precious
like Diamonds in Necklace
Momma soon settin you FREE
She's in ya Business
That's just How Family Be
She Lovin Her Seed
2008's A Diploma
Next comes A College Degree
But take time Slow
It's plenty to see
Each Day
Love who you Be
You're NEVER Alone
Check the Family Tree
Bling Bling
Shine on Forever

This is last words From My Voice
Life is Yours
Make the Most with each Choice
AND She Will

Cuz She's
Hannah Rossen Kopen
She Rises like Sunshine
13 and She's Flossin
Leavin the Past on A timeline
On Route to the Future
So chillax and unwind
It's hard to learn Hebrew
But Baby
You A Woman
So take your time,

29

OUR UNCHAINED MELODY

I see Symmetry and Words
And I want 2 Make them Dance

A Melody for Love

A Melody for Pain

A Melody to convince the World
Our Feelings are all the same.

San Miguel de Allende, 2005

fREe-RUN

STOP HOLDING ME!!!
Thatz simply my imagination running wild
Unpredictable thought-speed which I travel
In my own space and dialogue
Beyond the Brain-Bank of Fog

I THINK ahead
Often running behind

HOPING to even out in the end
While odd amends
Mend scarred slashed on my continual timeline
Prototype Backspine
From which you resigned

Trained measurements of envy
Calculate your re-active predictions of my actions
In Installments
Unfortunately, I don't have 6-8 weeks for deliveries
Your Official Handbook on civil obedience will
not reach me
SO PLEASE!
STOP HOLDING ME+BREATHE
CUZ FOR THE MOMENT
THATZ ONLY MY IMAGINATION RUNNING WILD!!!

TOO COOL TO PUT ON GLOVES

I'm staring at a blank white wall
Searching for colorful answers
Melodie whispers
Seep from the black speakers next to me
Slowly entering my ears
Piercing my drums with heavy beats
I'm laying on my back
Sinking between a couch and a hard place
I've been holdin this cordless plastic device 5 hours
Tryin to communicably understand nature's most
simple emotion
The problem is it's often so complex

Your voice resonates in my body
And sweet tones dial-up distant memories
Reminding me of love shared
Scared
Becuz our options aren't seeming optional

CLICK

And reality is unrealistic
I've arrived at a crossroads 10 years ahead of
schedule
And the light is yellow
Not blinking
About to turn red
Better think fast if I want it green
I'm low on gas

THINK
Gotta pay attention

PHONE RINGS/

"How are you?" she asks
Hidden behind an intricate web of dangling wires
"What'z on your mind?"

"Nothing" I respond
As my gas evaporates
And the light turns to blinking red
Cuz I'm now at the crossroad
About to make a nervous possibility optional
Due to our love shared

Through distant tones
That still manage to navigate a path
Directly through my phone jack and into my mind
Resulting in nature's most simple emotion
While I hide between a couch and a hard place
Staring at a blank white wall searching for
colorful awswerz

"You sure" she questions

"Yeh ..., I'm cool"

San Miguel de Allende, 2005

CLUB APOGEE

Club Apogee
The most distant point from Earth One might be
And it's here we meet
Suddenly
Feeling the heat
In drumming beat

I'm having a tranquil illusion.
Do you feel it wherever you are?
I'm feeding off your energy
Solo, In this bar

Alone in the spot right now
Hologram picture playin you next to me
Body Blessing B
Cranium Ecstasy
I love undressing We

Closing my eyes
I'm designing the poster
Cum closer
You're catching too much attention
I love and value our appreciative protection
I have the memories stored on collection
Put together like a puzzle
And guarded with my SOUL weapon

If you choose, I've left a trail of tears for you
To trek the river here
I'll float the clouds until your near
Waiting patiently at
Club Apogee
The most distant point from Earth where One might be

FEELINGS

Do you take your emotions on walks
Ridicule or pet them when they talk
Let them roam free, when there is room to move
comfortably
Do they live in peace
OR
Are they on a tight leash

Do you let your emotions run you
Do they shun you
Or

Do you control them
Playing games and feeding them
Rewarding or breeding them

Do they get the best of you
Do they jest at you
Or Hopefully,
At the end of the Night
Do they curl at the foot of the bed and rest with you

A FREE SEX DIAMOND

U SEE YOUR UNIVERSAL LANGUAGE
EXPRESSING RHYTHM
IN DELICIOUS SHINING SMILES

A LIP HONEY
MY LIQUID CANDY
SPRAYING POETRY HEAD TO BLOOD

A PINNACLE FEELING OF JOY IS WHAT YOU REMIND ME OF
DRINKING FRESH AIR IN YOUR VELVET GARDEN
A PRISONER 2 THE DEEP PERFUME
SCENTED BY REGAL INSIGHT
IT IS AS IF THE BREEZE YOU DELIVERED HAS INSTANTLY
MANIFESTED THE REASON OF MY ENTIRE DAY

SHOWING HUMILITY AT THE GATE OF NATURE
EVERY BLUSH INVITING YOUR RAW JUICE
CONCENTRATING, I WATCH
A LOVELY BARE GODDESS DANCE

CLOSER, I MOVE
MY TONGUE GENTLY LICKS THE FLOWER
FINGERING HER DELICATE PETALS OF SEASONED PURITY
REMEMBERING ALWAYS NOT TO MANIPULATE YOU

A FREE
SEX
DIAMOND

SUNRISE, SUNSET

I met the sun yesterday
She crept daringly behind my ear
Whispering heated images
Echoes massaging my scalp
She sprayed light Rays upon my solid spirit
Permeating the pores of my imagination
I stopped briefly to absorb

I absorbed the sun today
And my body filled with strength
And in the beauty of her shine
I became addicted to her spine
A rare loyalty in my vision of ephemeral reality
Tell me why our galaxies
Connected
Our Blooming Growth
But why in my first orbit of time
Because I already know
Tonight the Sun will set

San Miguel de Allende, 2005

Tomorrow the Sun will rise and rain warmth upon
her path
An invisible lovebath
My own spine now tingles from the reaction
of her embrace
Hoping to digest all the heat. Face to Face
I know I may not see the sun forever
As seasons are not an eternal guarantee
Although somewhere I know the warmth will always burn
This is felt
Quite certainly
You see
She was never a one night glow
And so

Our spiritz have connected
For the eternity of life to come

And she will always be beside me
The Beauty of My Sun

THE PROLETARIAT CHARIOT

(Unfinished)

I love ridin' public
Proletariat Chariot
Even if realistic
Ya gotta witness & deal wit dumb stuff
People erked, sad, high or trippin'
But flip-side are the meditators
Deep in thought outta window
Reading and flippin'

It's like the Discovery Kingdom
For mammals truly livin'
I love to dip in, sit down and fit in.
I love ridin' public
Spectrum of cultures, classes & religions
Packed next to each other
Back to back like that's it...
No VIP's cuz on public

We all brothers
Deal with it
Hot or cold
Stuck en route
Young & old, nobody has more clout
Test of patience...
Cuz you're late for work
& without fail, the biker can't
get the bike rack to work.

I love public
Because in here we're all equal
Bus driver don't like you

Or any other people
Be calm & enjoy the emotions
Listen to the conversations
Or not
Plug in your earbuds
& sip the visual lot
Fashion show on your parade
A constantly evolving Float

So enjoy...hold on tight & try to cope
Pray the seats are cotton
Look outside & watch the flowers blossom

You're on public
The Proletariat Chariot

San Miguel de Allende, 2005

MY WOMAN

I WANT A LANE BRYANT WOMAN, A NON-COMPLIANT
NEVER SILENT
WOMAN

A SPEAK HER OWN, INDEPENDENT TONE,
LEAVE ME THE FUCK ALONG
TYPE WOMAN

San Miguel de Allende, 2005

A PICK UP THE CHECK, NO DISRESPECT,
SHAKES FOR A KID ON THE NECK
TYPE WOMAN

I WANT A LOVE IS SUPREME, SHOWERS THE TEAM,
WALK IS MEAN
TYPE WOMAN

I WANT A CASUALLY DRESSED,
PREFERS PEACE OVER STRESS, PUT HER
HEAD ON YOUR CHECT
TYPE WOMAN

CUZ YOU KNOW YOU WANT ALL THREE
AND THATZ MY TYPE OF WOMAN

A LOVE AND HAPPINESS, TAKE A BATH AND KISS,
EMITS A SIMPLE BLISS
TYPE WOMAN

I WANT A TELEPATHIC FOREPLAY,
SHADOWS MY BRAINWAVES, FIND ME
IN LIFES LOVEMAZE
TYPE WOMAN

N' SHIT
THATZ MY TYPE OF WOMAN
SO GO GET YOUR OWN

LET ME SAY,
AT THE RISK
OF SEEMING
RIDICULOUS,
THAT THE
TRUE
REVOLUTIONARY
IS GUIDED
BY GREAT
FEELINGS
OF LOVE

DÉJEME DECIRLE, A RIESGO DE PARECER RIDÍCULO, QUE EL REVOLUCIONARIO VERDADERO ESTA GUIADO POR GRANDES SENTIMIENTOS DE AMOR

Max's favorite poster, always on display wherever he lived.

2

R U MAD?

POLITICS AND
THE CHALLENGE OF NOW

Drawing, Max Monroy-Miller

ACT NOW!!!

THE TIME IS NOW
THE FUTURE STANDS HERE
HOW MANY CLICHES COULD MAKE IT MORE CLEAR
LEAVE THIS POEM AND BUY RIOT GEAR
REVOLUTION IS NOT AN ACT OF FEAR
IT SHOULD BE ON YOUR RESUME TO CHANGE CAREERS

R U MAD?

I'm mad and do you want to know why
I was roofied and date-raped by fate
She forced my mistakes
And said she was teaching me a lesson
Beginning of my confidence compression
Downward spiral to depression
Guilt-ridden and blaming myself
Rather than You
Like I-O-U
Why O—U?
YOU
But I own me
We
The poisoned bodies of Voyagers Venom
Seeking and Antidote to release the toxins
Feelin- boxed in — And that is why I'm mad
Question is — R U?
Highly evolved
Now Highly Disolved
In a post 9/11
Slow regression of Freedom
Our Blood Bleedin'
We're dyin, like a hairline recedin'
Trust me, I've taken Yoga for reasons
R U Mad?

I'm posin a question to you
Tell me your truth
Can you articulate your grief
Long or Brief
Do you live externally — Raisin' your hand to speak
Survive Superficially

Self-Worth measured materialistically
Living unaware in subtle captivity
Heir to a cycle of misery
Disillusioned Tranquility
Lost in a Vanilly Sky
Tech support says we're a bad Chicano Play right now
Been acting in a plummeting script
Self-producin' White Power Productions Directionial Debut
Trippen and Fallen Right on Cue

Steppin Fetchits you
Sanded and Stripped
Conditioned and Stainwashed
But not completely Brainwashed
Too Deep — Peep!!!
15th century Cortes says
"There were even officials in charge of sweepin'"
1,000 public workers maintainin Tenochititlan streets N'
Cortes wrote it — So I quote it
Original Antithesis to a dirty Mexican
Does that Medicate the Myth they've kept us in
Eat. It's Medicine
30 minutes in the American Holocaust is the dust
I sniffed it in

Now R U Mad
Cuz there's hours more
To the foundational Core
Blatant Data Alteration
Conservative and liberal manipulation
With a one dimensional implementation
Intellectual thievery — Repeatedly —

INHALE!!!
Urban Sprawl gone AWOL.
And they still cuttin' trees.
Natural Disaster Disease
When they sell our oxygen and respiratories cease
Then, when Breath is Currency
Will you feel the urgency
To speak more critically
Think analytically
Then would you be Mad?

Latent warriors!!
Would you be mad if you knew you were in a pool of
potential energy
Complacently Ignoring Synergy
Latrines of a Capitalist Policy
How many flocks can you see?
A population of followers disgustin me
Short-term actors serving long-term purposes
Purposeless
It's only Your Energy They Utilize
Super Sized French Fries
Stop playin Bad Guys
Unwise to the Disguise
If I'm wrong...Then will the leaders rise!!!
Hidin behind the curtain of closed eyes

Rogue Cries
And hump necks
So I'm wonderin'
Straight up and down – who'll be next
Who'll read between the line and ignore the text
Are you foolish enough to believe
That Malcolm and Martin are the victims of random rejects

Or that ol' boy at Enron really committed suicide
outta deep stress
WTC bombings are only pretext

Do you believe money is not a plague
Is this becoming too vague, too raw, or too clear
Must I draw back so you'll come near
Perhaps, too distant, although blinded by this spotlight
I see your shadow, sadly following your flesh,
completely unaware
You see me too, don't front a glare
We're both positioned on the edge
They sing our requiem in synchronized tones
I've paid money at a museum to see my own ancestors bones
Does it seem so historical
The stolen gold
Do we really still think we're not bought and sold
Business Colleagues got you on a corporate conveyor belt
In with the fresh brains, out with the old
Brain mold
SO It's time to ante up. Don't fold
Cuz I'm no different, just discoverin my role
I'm also a gold tooth victim
Slave to a system
Whose mother is a market
Rolled out by Kings with Red Carpet
Growin Weary of Acceptin the norm
Holdin a green rose, bein' poked by its thorn

Now, at this point, have my thoughts struck you odd
In the midst of all this confusion, does God?
What is your feeling' on Drug Dealin'?
Does it disintegrate our youth? What's the proof?
Remember, I want personal truth

Sharp or Uncouth
Is it me smoking crack that should have you scared
Cuz knowin how broke the hood it, how'd it get there?
It's called big-time entrapment
The government creates vices that require remedies
Police be the middle man enemy

They rarely protect or serve anything
Beyond the investments and interests of their master.
Think Faster
And Colored Cops. STOP
They granted you a degree in the acquisition of ephemeral
power
You incarceratin your own culture in showers
With Batons, Bulletproof and Pistol
Shatter our spirits of Fine Crystal
Drivin through the 'hood on a homemade houseslave pedestal
Fact that the plantation transformed and survived is
unbelievable
N' the worst ain't the Long Bidz
Life skidz
Itz the Kids
Hearing misguided messages
So here's my declaration slash anthem
If a pig violates you — reach back as hard as you can and
smash' em
Reshape his pudgenose face
Their haste makes waste
Time we throw the book and they crack our case
True Bad Boys protectin' the interest of the system
They're the pawns and we're the victims
Justified through Bible manipulation
A book translated multiple times
I exposed it through multiple rhymes

Neighborhood watch need to start cuffin these blues up
for multiple crimes.

Am I mad? Hell Yeah!!
What state are you in?
A state of denial
Ignorant, bitter and sad
Doesn't that make you mad?
Led Astray
Paving their Corporate Way
Piston of their strength
Paying money for a CEO to form your desires and tastebuds
Digitize and document your exploitation
Then offering sanitization in direct forms of restoration
But all that's happening is you keep giving
Years keep loving
WERE YOU?
Constantly Consuming the produce
Imagine, it's 2020 and the product has been renamed
"self-mutilation'
Don't get red or front humiliation
You know you're gonna be the first to buy it.
Six different colors and sizes
Awwww...Does my dispassionate prediction make you mad?

Does it make you mad that somehow their ends always
justify their means
For example, the government created blame
What were you sayin?
Should be renamed Action Tame
See, In his panic the plan was devised
Still recovering, we were hypnotized
They never sincerely heard our cries
Or Maybe cuz you were silent

Compliant
A living Acronym
H. omogenous. I. nsecurities. S. olidified. P. repackaged
A. merican. N. ulllifying. I. ndegenous C. ulture
AKA HISPANIC
That Panics
I've banned it
Not Janet
And by now, I know you think this song is about you.

We're buying food stamped dangerous
Kuntageous
Patented and Patterned for all ages
I'm boycottin' unhealthy products in stages.
Assemblin' my autobiography in pages
Chapter 11 to blaze myths
Filed Bankruptcy on propaganda distractions
Ignoring media contraptions in contractions
We are the consequences of Bush's Actions
Abusive misuse of Democracy
File it under mockery
With Capitalist Complementaries
For Too many Centuries
In Swarms like Bees
Get Mad so WE CAN GET FREE

Cuz I am tired of being the talented player
with no Coach
I ignore the chime of our requiem
My last finger slipping is glued to the pendulum
Measuring our time
Cuz I Am Not A Holiday
I am Not A Latin EXPLOSION
I am NOT A PARADE

I am NOT Your Song used to Serenade
I will no longer be played
Been Mad since first grade
I hated when all the kids obeyed

Doesn't make me misbehaved
Just a moral duty to question the hypocrisy of Authority
Cuz a Blind perception is all Bad
So for the last time, R U Mad????

Then get up and say it!!
I don't care if you speak through religion
Pray it
NEW TASK
Real world Cast
We're gonna make up for time past
From now on, When they Hike, We PASS
Fuck a draft
Do the Aztec Math
Embrace your Native Past
On sale for Free
Wrote this poem in the MSU Library
Finished February 15th at 2:43
Love writin mad poems like therapy
Anger Management literally
And if you felt half of me
Or one line, let it digest and be
Cuz even if 95% were satisfied
4% were sad
And 1% were all we had
The D.A. could Flip it
And D-A-M
DAM
I'd still be MAD!!!!!!

Max at the Aztec
Sun Stone, National
Anthropology
Museum, Mexico City

TEOTIHUACAN

12/28/00

Aqui,
With the Moon upon me
Entering me
I withdraw my attention
Broadening perceptions of misinterpretations
Staring with green eyes de maguey
I am able to absorb my own thoughts
Drinking down every last drop of pulque
The Avenue of the Dead suddenly awakens
The Merchants like Cacti are at full bloom
Children running like the Jaguar
Stretching their cries upwards
To the clouds that wash away their tears
Tlaloc is always listening to his seeds
The elderly sit perched upon nests of weathered rock
Knowing it is their time to rest
They have flown this land 360 degrees
Defining persistence and soon will fly again
The nature of cycles awaits their entrance

Aqui,
With the Sun spraying energy upon me
I close my eyelids and recharge
Knowing the warmth will find me
Believing the rays permeated my flesh long ago
I am dressed lightly, even on the coolest day
And as Quetzalcoatl sleeps before me
I am reminded of a time preserved in Heart.
He moves to remind me the feeling is real
And I smile
Aqui.

RECOGNITION

I'm Fed up and Spoiled
I need to cut my arteries
Containing your hate and misogyny
Inevitably a part of me
Drain your institutional ideologies
The American Influence that deceitfully jumpstarted me
Strain my membrain to eliminate the mindstate of your
oppressive whiteology
Walking cancerous
All my people susceptible
And your entrance has just been diagnosed as Historiez
most feared epidemic
An outbreak Virus
And you know America won't support a free Clinic

I used to want harmony
Peace for all people
Joined hands across America
Thought we could all be equal
But the longer I sit in this shade you perceive as sun
The more difficult I find it to sympathize as ONE.

Now immune 2 ideas of equality
Becuz ironically we think we're Free
So Fuck Aidz – I don't even want my body
And Fuck America too – Cuz they have let our souls rot
internally
So I'm gonna cut my arteries
Cuz I don't want the mold that is part of me
Hang me upside down
And drain your evil thoughts to the ground
Mother Earth will break them down

Laugh now but when you lay your eyes
She'll still be around
Polluted with bad weather
On Tums trying to digest and swallow you clowns

You Crackerz don't want to solve problems
Too unreasonably pragmatic
Tracked it back to your demographic
Realized through your lens greed is systematic
Patriarchial Religious Fanatics

Abusing a Spirit to gain battle tactics
Arriving here without reservations
Cuz yours were not properly granted
God Damn IT!!!!
Him too!
Killed him on a cross
Praise Him when he's lost
Expect us to understand the Mental Fog
Let me Pause

Return to my thoughts
Got caught up again in yours
And Notice – Got Lost

So drain my Internal
Burn it eternal
And Reconstruct
Start from the Toes and move up
Then take a Million More People of COLOR
And line them up

POW'S ARE MIA

Is N E one else concerned that our POW's R MIA
Is N E one else concerned that our elders may have
gone astray
Cuz in case you weren't aware our Xicano Nation
is still at war,
And in case you didn't know we're fighting for even more
Your children are still dying
Often at the command of our own brown faces
In fact, the numbers are increasing
And I'm getting frustrated that our POW's R MIA
spiritually deceasing

Did your Brown Pride die when you joined the
Corporate Best
I got nervous
So itz tattooed upon my chest
Red, White and Green over my heart to remind me
to the death

Did your Brown Pride die with Royalties
When you published your first book
Or did you just give up cuz you forgot what
"Viva La Raza"
really took.

Your MIA cuz I can't find your trace
Your MIA cuz you forgot the challenges your legacies
would face
And this is not a relay where you simply pass us the Baton
This is not wizardry where you wave a magic wand
This is a continuum of Revolution and I'm upset
Cuz our POW's R MIA and the job is still not done

I've read your names on paper and wondered where
you went
I see the dangling fruits of Xicano Labor
Respecting the struggles of time well spent
But don't give me any excuses cuz we all got Bills and rent

And you won't claim insurance from me
Security is not free
So if you thought retirement was in "El Plan"
You betta read anotha copy

So I'll leave it with you Cold and Real
Cuz it'z time for direct action
And I'm scared where my own path leads
If my POW's are still missing in Action

FREESTYLE VISIONS
OF DEC. 31, 2000 (PUEBLA)

Paleteria Cart, Red-White and Green Confetti, Cowboy
Hat, Jesus Statue, Green Leaves, Faces of Wet Adobe,
Chants of "Chicle, Chocolate, Dulce-Dos Pesos!", Brooms
made of Recycled Branches Sweeping Remnants
of Fallen Tortillas, Indigenous Hearts Painting the
Sidewalk-Detached from a soil-separated by a broken
rock that no longer protects – but Disconnects,
Distorted images of Faith Preserved in spaces where
doors run on Schedules, Who needs Confession?
Anahuac Gods existent through markets and Vendors,
Sadly engraved on Ashtrays – the Butt of Anglo Jokes,
Cell Phones, Police sirens, and screams of Elote. Bells
that ring in memory of Tyranny, 3 year old Brown
Warriors that marvel at simplicity, Fountains that have
been sprayin for Centuries, Mosaics, Talaveras, Chalupas,
y Coronas, Taxi Bugs, Taquerias, and ATM's. Broad
Noses, White Skin, Blue Eyes, Pointed Noses, Brown
Skin, Autumn Thighs, Nahuatl Voices echo laughter in
passing. Tiendas de Nueva Espana, Brown eyes peering

over Golden Arches waiting for Value Meals while the meals that should be valued are outside in the Zocolo for half the price, Price of Preservacion, Recycle Trash Cans on every corner — still ahead of their time. Fake Gold for tourists Cuz The Cathedral is saving Yellow Walls for Religious Fashion Shows, Army of Salvation guards the Fortress Doors and the Salvation Army, well, they are Here. Here, Existent in smiles of Lovers who Hold Hands Mirroring their fathers through Black Obsidian as they Pass Time. Black Moustaches, Fully Developed Panzas, Initialed Belt Buckles and Kickers, A child sleeping peacefully in one arm, their Corazon tightly embraced in the other. Work Ethic. Family Values. Grandma, Grandpa, Mother, Daughter, Father, Son – Walking and Talking of their Dayz Thawtz. Grandma, Grandpa, Mother, Daughter, Father, Son sitting quietly next to the street sign thinking their Thawtz. Unity. Respect. Culture so Rich you can only absorb one Bite at a Time to Fully Absorb the Beauty. And Proudly I Feast.

San Miguel de Allende, 2005

UNITED GATES OF AMERIKA

United Gates of Amerika
Is our dilution
Your solution
Like waterin' down juice
Our nutrients dissolve through a slow execution
People treated like pollution
Market and media boostin
Sections of our culture
Like a vulture
You prey on our brown meat
Infiltrate and rape
Proud to mistreat
Destroyed our culture and still you hate
I gotta get it off my chest man
One time in a proactive stance
I could forgive 'em – nah, not a chance!
My system is boiling over
I'm sittin dull in a class filled with ignorant minds
Perpetuating the racism of our times
Eurocentric showers
White rain devours – my skin like a snake
I shed and bend
Contend my views. Kneeled in pues
Prayin to a god lyin in pink and purple hues
Oooooooohhh!!!
And with time ticking I grow angry
Insanity cripples my soul
My thoughts are trapped deep below
If I can't break free, I'm destined to blow
My ribs are gonna split
Surge through my chest

Down my arms until I split your Shhhhhh...
We could live peacefully but it seems you don't want me
to quit
You perpetuate the legacy of exploitation
"If you ain't of my persuasion, well..."
You've done it all
Scientifically producing solutions
saying our craniums were Mathematically smaller
based on metric calculations and racism
stemming From your condemning nation
Now Let's travel the road for those who seem to
Swim in shallow water
paddlin away at the mouth — satisfied with their Wealth
Can't blame you for not understanding me
Huh – you don't even understand yourself
If we look into our past, you'll find that you feared your own
Left your home, and land in search of something more grand
NOTICE!!!
YOU CAME HERE
We had no plans to look for you, not becuz we were savage
But we had no reason to
Then after you stole what you could have just shared
You showed your true colors and got lazy
Went to Africa, and denied my man his history
Historians data seems hazy....hmmmmmm
You trace everything back
Weren't you proud of that attack?
Is that why my friends can't trace their origins or ancestry
Geneology trees
Branches burnin' like leaves

500 years have passed since you initiated this
united bloodbath
And what is your claim
Mad — when I connect you to this shame.
Credit it to your name
Say we're minorities but that ain't the case cuz that
is a title
and no one Labels me idle
And now my conscious thoughts evolve in tiny strands
That sprout from my scalp and fall short of performance
They got us making decisions indecisively
Government gives freedom of thought stipends
Corporate culprit Americans ripen
Original thought frightens
Our social construction tightens
We could live others dreams but what about our own
Our ribs have become the gates of a prison entrapping a
beautiful we
We have subjugated our own intelligence
Hence
The foundation, for our creation
Is facing deterioration

BUT WAIT!!!!!!!!!!!!

Give me time
To express the bottom line
In this timeframe designed
Witness our reality
500 years strong is the claim in every town
They say we are detrimental to society with our violent
statistics
And ghettos rundown
Son, we built it all

Black and Brown
It's time we educate 'em, cuz we'll tear it right back down
But first do the mathematics and check the historical patterns
That determine our status
We were both robbed of land and brutally murdered
Both beaten and denied time to recover
Both built the infrastructure that denies us our rights
Both forced to withstand time and keep the family tight
Now out of 500 years of blood and frustration
Have you any idea how long we were denied education
Not to mention, our form of communication is even Caucasian
But I'm not too mad, just hear our word and try to understand
The experience we had
It's been a few decades of legal participation
Compared to 470 years of Americas racial segregation
Now look me in the eye and say that I'm slow
You don't wanna do that
Cuz I won't say excuse me when I step on those toes

They pretend to incorporate us within their system, however,
That's not a reward
LISTEN!!!!

That is an evolutionary aspect of their personal agenda
Subordinatin our cultures
Claimin' Multi-culturalism to blend ya'
As they continue the idea of modern day slavery
We are doin' in a pinch of time
What they were given from 15-1-9

So let me praise this Brown and Black nation
For my people of color
I'll be there
No hesitation

SAVE THE KIDS

Yo, Big Moe was caught up in Subconscious
Strangle Holds
My Misdemeanor
I Never Told 'em Fold
But what I saw. I let 'em know
Don't B Fooled by Name Brands
They Stain Man
Trends Deceive and Recycle Friends
Naked — Our Hearts Blend
Shot From Magic Bags — To Remove the Mask
of Plastic Tags
We've Traveled From Rags — To Rich
And Rich — Right back to Rags
Now Slave Lynchings Sag From Droopy Chins
Of Spoiled Kin and We Grown Men
Still Grumpy Within
See Few Heroes Bound to Win
Cuz Majority of Potential Corporate Destined
Cuz Minds like Mine Been Studyin too Long
And Mouths alike been Quiet entire Songs

Inhalin' Bongs. Captive to Thongs.
And Admittedly, I was Wrong
But Eternally, Time Moves On
A Starting Line Appears Wherever You Begin
Whenever, You Choose to Amend
And Patiently Waitin, Are Seeds Deservin Gems
Ready for Our Shinin' Rays
We Must Tend to Them B-4 Their Led Astray
Together, We'll Wed this Style at Future Births
Fightin Imbalance for Everything it's Worth
Love Thirsts, So Love Always Comes First
And With Future Worth
Big Moe Accepts Who He Can Still Become
Realizes He Can Recycle Life and Help the Young
Some Gifts in Life are Destined Son

And Now, When Moe see's Youth
He gives Pounds
Like Peace
And One

Drawing, Max Monroy-Miller

3

WHISPER SCREAMZ

ADDICTION AND STRUGGLES

Drawing, Max Monroy-Miller

ALONE

I preferred 2 live my momentz
In the company of others
But indifferent 2 my feelings
She appeared, void of any others

She is the silence
In Quiet Hours
When No One is Near You

She is also the Fears
With Whispering Powers
That Flashes Past the Rearview

Eventually, As Time Persisted
Rejection Became a Chore
So I began 2 Accept her Relentless Pursuit
Inviting Solitude In my Door
I extended my hand 2 the lonely Space
I felt the Nothing and Embraced it
Slowly, we began 2 dance
Following the moments of her Greatness
I grabbed nervously around her memories
She blinked and led me into our synergy

Then Suddenly
With the Wind, Our Second wind Was met with
Peaceful Chimes
And this connection indirectly made the music mine

Without a Word
Without a Sound
A lonely heart began 2 pound

She took my Hand and Pulled me Close
With a final Dip...I proposed a toast

To who I am
To who I'll B
I thank my soul...For accepting Me

TIRED

In past sense
Mistakes have helped shape me
Presently
With strong belief
I wanna cut back on them greatly

Rudy's Can't Fail Cafe, Emeryville, Calfornia.

ONE MILLISECOND LEFT

What will appear
When the Shadow is here
Will I fear the mirror of my Last Blink?
What will be caught In my Final Thawt?
What memory will I be left 2 think?

And what for the sinz that are scars within
Will my calls for forgiveness breed a calming satisfaction
Will there B time to say I'm sorry for all my careless actions
If truth hold value, they never mimicked my intentions
So, will you please Kiss me goodbye As I slowly lose
my Vision

I am afraid 2 die
Behind my eyes
Trapped in pain
Opposed 2 risen

TRUE FRAGRANCE

First poem, 1999

Fragrance of false energies
Breezes through air
Unfair
Leaving man, womyn and child trapped in purple
blood capsules
Of endless despair

Me is the object
I project
To interject the LUV and HATE we feel

Metal is the hard state of Hate
Compounded
Leaving me Dumbfounded
With negative vibez
Twitch off that
And you thought this shit was easy

Beauty still abundant
So I proclaim myself free
Havin found that last drop of love in my faucet
Givin' me the strength to carry further

But fleeces of Hate
Insulate
The devil sword and again I'm trapped
Down and down
Drowning in that well-known but ignored abyss
My mind spits fears like STD's in piss

Deceived again by the mark of the beast

Then BOOM!!!
I perceived the light of my shadow calling
CHOKED
Blue in Death

But I switch your perception and say
Blue
Like the color of sky that becumz my limitless hope
And again I breathe My True Fragrance

San Miguel de Allende, 2005

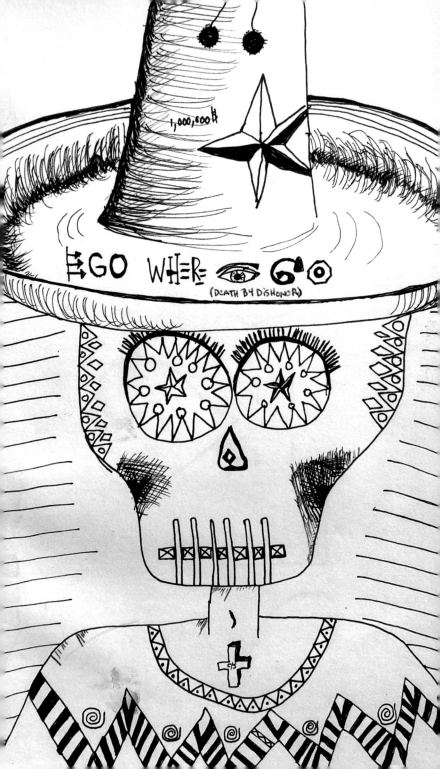

MY INDOOR VOICE

December 27, 2004

From Within it Trembles
Then Echoes under the moonlight
So a compromise is settled
When you awaken to the daylight

And Time, Time is just a circle
Reminders by the elderly and children
Thawtz and feelings to be hurdled
So am I versed, and now immersed in

And if your mind resorts to sadness
The strength of soul can override the pain
Vice Versa is the Antidote of Opposite
Loosen now, Nature cannot B explained

So my Heart beats slower
My senses Blend and Guilt is not for shame
I am truth in Spirit, Love in SOUL And a power that
chooses to B unnamed

And When From Within It Trembles
I take Openhanded at the Palm
Where a Compromise is Settled
And I breathe Joy into the DAWN

EMBRYO MONOLOGUE

I infinitely wake up
To bake up
4:36 in the morning
Routinely, Me and old Birdz Caked up
With the snow cone A+
Yells my attention and she shakes rough

I'm facing Death Row Prostitution
Sacred Womb Execution
Planted Solution
Mixed me into the ring of Life
Closed Sound Surrounded
Vulnerable to Vein taps pounded
Young innocence to a crime getting grounded

BUT I AM
Destiny's Child
A SOUL Survivor

With Relentless Whispers
That shook the rock away from Jesus's CaveDoor
A Body that MOCKS Sin from the TombCore
A Guinea Pig of the governments Pharmaceutical System
Forced to Rest in
Crackin up of these premeditated cosmic lessons
WHERE'S MY WISH AND FORTUNE
I was bondaged and forced in
Undeveloped lips suppressed my right to question
THE ONLY CHOICE IN TIME WHERE THEY HEISTED
MY DECISION!!!!

Inebriated, Incarcerated
Selfishly Hated
And Knotted up, unaware
Fortunately, I escaped quietly with only a heart murmur
to share
Sharing your reflection of selfish Tastes
Buds, Poked needles and Base — Luv
Yeah, That's the uncovered truth
I was Domestic Drugged

It'z a miracle the Umbilical Rope doesn't Lynch me
The Hooked angel silently raped by pimp bea(s)ts

But I'm fightin my re-creation with bigger feats
I broke outta jail for a pinch a PEACE

Foundational Film rips off like Maybeliene
Runnin Free and Washed Clean
Everyday I wake up your next dream
The living reincarnation of yesterdays tears
and there's a 50/50 chance my smiles hid fears
Regardless
I am Here
Sharing just the articulation of my Embryo Monologue
A Therapeutic Dialogue
To defrost y'all
misCONCEPTION fog

WASTING MY TIME

My dreams Exist
Hibernating in the shadows of my Nightmares
My Life Persists
Awakening to the Solitude of Blank Stares

And WHO Cares
And WHO Cares

A 20/20 Blur
Frozen Passion Staring Back in the Mirror
Realizations gradually incurred
A confused Hopelessness draws nearer

And These R My Fears
And These R My Fears

I suppose this creates an Ambiguity to my
Self Description
The reason some days are in control and other
Breaths get Lost
Character Indecisiveness Diagnosed as my affliction
Meanwhile Moods Swing and Signals Cross

And in the Meantime, I tend to Flatline

And Time is often Lost
And Time is often Lost
And time
Is
Often
Lost

Drawing, Max Monroy-Miller

WHISPER SCREAMZ

I Whisper Screamz
And Explode with Laughter
A ray of light that shatterz humyn Plaster
I am Sun
I am Moon
I set brightly
And then rise with Echoes of Pain
My strength is consumed
By Missionaries of Hate
If I were not my own worst enemy
You would easily see the beauty of me
But I grow weak with experience
The more I see the less I care
Wondering subconsciously who decided this was fair

My body is a rock
Solid Within
Trapped
I want to burst like a bubble and escape
But my skin has become impenetrable
So I keep walking
Walking
Walking
And I end up nowhere

My friend says I am Yellow
PURE
And that people don't take the time to come near
Do Friends really listen?
They have pre-determined instincts
That reject the ability to think
We constantly react and give answers
Riddles that swarm and grow like cancer
A destructive force that misguides people
We never seem to learn
We just repeat thoughts

When I screamed help I was caught
So I no longer Blend my yellow
I've learned to hold me inside and harden
I see you in passing and nothing has changed
Cuz I still whisper screamz and explode with laughter

CONDENSED DOWN

Condensed Down to a singular crowd
I read Allowed
Pages tearing from my eye
I tend to speak my cry

Do you enforce what you believe in
Do you breathe in
Are you waitin to exhale
Or just appeasing'
I'm lonely sometimes, just easin'
Walkin like the leanin tower of pisa
N' I can't ever please' em
Thinkin itz straight

But I see how everything around you
Grows, go's, passes and replants
Shake it, Can't
Chance, Scant
The experiences generally stick
And We've been informed to learn directly from our teachin
Some look in, some adhere to preachin
Some struggle to balance
Non-violence or violence
Rebellion or compliance
In other words, Acceptance or defiance
Seen too many cast out in silence
So I scream for our voice to be heard BEEN called absurd
Heavy Word
By the Hummingbird
Who never seems to listen or pay attention

Not just to what I'm spitten
Oral or written
But to my movement and dance
My beat, my trance
My stance, my Romance

You constantly keep judging me to hear your own answer
Posted like the GZA's sho-gun decapitator
Spirit Evaporator
Deadlier than Darth-Vader
Seem Incapable of Appreciating styles
So like JOE, you remain a hater

And through it all
I'm still deciphering when to bite my tongue
Or choose my battles
The world is starving for people that think for themselves
If the supply is low, demand is high
Economic Fact, But it's surfaced a lie
So am I truly locked in — Like John Q
Systemz Milked Me — and You
True Patriotz,
With Strong Potency Potentially
Tired of tasting my misery
In definitions of modern prosperity — Sincerily
Barely dodging the warp channels of Deceptive Imbecility
Neglecting the subconscious addict who
follows mobbocracy
In the quiet explosions of my mind, Dead Prez still
gets me free
A Reminding Relief

So could we change Relativity for Morality
Would it travel see's
Dispel fallacies
Could a gust of wind change the direction of our future
Could the velocity re-root ya
If our emotional portholes could feel souls
Would you Switch roles
Does Freedom really wave from flagpoles
When I'm scared

I often troll goals
Need Insoles
For rough roads and potholes
Too many obstacles and loopholes

And while time is slowly digested
I realize the results of what I've invested
My foggy lens, then, attempts to mend
But the truth is I want to be young again

Why is it only in the middle ages of life that we pretend
we're not kids nomore

Excuse me. I don't mean to bore
But It's only so often the mask exposes the sore
And only so much I can really let pour
I've been runnin up my mind
Meter needs deposits and emptyin to fuel more time
Been ridin this train so long to keep foundin' what I find

San Miguel de Allende, 2005

Of course, Voice Horse
I'm speakin to my own grind
But I'd guess occasionally we're both bein' defined
Perhaps one day, they'll realize they can't decipher me
at will anymore
They'll call me crazy, for sure
Therefore While I'm still regarded as publicly sane
I'll keep feeling,
Attempting to explain

Cuz for a moment
Condensed down to a singular crowd
I read — Allowed
Pages tearing from my eye
I tend to speak my cry

CONVO WITH MIRROR

I was alone in my mind when I heard my soul whisper

"Don't discount your sense. You're wondering when
It's right and time is slowly Wasting your life. Hoping
for a flashing light — to turn you on. Hiding behind
Transparent bars. Trapped by your pain, paralyzed by
Your scars. Who'll set you free?"

Who'll set you free

I turned around and thought
You just watch and see
Ironically, at this instant another opportunity was
pacin in me
A conversation with echoes of eternity

And then again, he interrupted
Quoting word
Asked me If I was waitin for a dream deferred

At first the Blunt-ness paralyzed my wordz
But aroused — I preferred
To speak more clearly and ensured

Sir
I see your message and must now confess this
I'm no longer stagnant
I hybridize my lessons
Organize directions
True
At a period of time
I was blind
But now I choose to make love with my time

He asked again, "But if you bumped into hope
and she offered you Life, would you
Believe it?"

Sir, I'm constantly offered chances
Listen how I perceive it

Alone in my room the lighter sparks
Where I diagram dimlit clouds filled with illusions
And sift thru the dark to boost my seclusion
In this timezone I find resolution
Standing idle behind confusion
Becuz the evolution of my mind
Tends to contradict itself often
Sitting here I find myself
Intricately lost in
Nomadic shadows
Disguised as varying perspectives

Yes, I know, it sounds reckless
But it's growth
So I continue to hybridize
Molding my reality to realize
Time is evolution and evolution is time maximized
I accept this in my battlecry
Not to remain a victim of past lives
I'm in that stage of development
Where I'm choosing what to sanitize

Then suddenly
He opened his eyes and nodded wise
I was now staring at his own reflection
Swimming across a placid mirror
Attempting to save me from drowning in myself
So I concluded aloud and offered my wealth

I'm accepting peace as perfect balance
I make mistakes and will be challenged
This is a test that can be managed
Enjoying mental anarchy where time is irrelevant
A cycle for me
Inner freedom
My acceptance of self-responsibility
Respecting the worlds complexity
My passion for life
My relentless dream

MAY-B

I would like 2 think
Time won't shrink
I'm Aware Thatz not the case
So, I wright to imagine of wrighting my wrongz
And push not 2 waste my space

I dream that History may love my soul
Living each Breath in Double-Pull
Yet, in the act of No Regretz
I breed Regretz
Over-eating when I should B Full

I pray that time will strain the Guilt
That Burns and Echoes in ones Heart
And Perhaps in the Dim I'll breath Again
And B delivered Another Start

UNTITLED

What truly flights you?
What reignites you?
Who is your prison guard?

When you drowned your tears are they buried far?
Do you dream of a life in stars?
Are your windows barred?
Enough questions
Life is hard.

San Miguel de Allende, 200?

I'M SO SAD

I am sad to not have lifelong friends that are physically close like you see in movies. I always wanted that. What can I do to create more community again in my life? I want to be in touch with the feeling of God breathing in and out of my lungs. Help people more consistently. Think of others frequently. Be content with being normal, one of many. My ego drives this terminal need to stand out in life. Let go of that fear of not being unique and just know God will determine my course if I listen.

THE DIRTY ANIMAL

I'm the dirty animal in the back of your mind
The one who comes out in poetry givin a fuck if I rhyme

I'm the sneeze plasterin your skin
I'm the same bug you see again and again
The ones you crush are only clones of my children.
I'm built in.
I'm everything you detest
I'm the dirty strip club breast
Feeding milk to the children who need it most
I'm the cristal toast
I'm the nasty thought that scarred the host
I'm the dark alley, flickering with broken street light posts
I'm the invisible ghosts
Cuz the indecent images are just scapegoats
Related and created to guard your fears
Come near
Cuz, In reality it'z me who got you shook
My brother keeps burning candles
Look, look, I'll tell you look
Cuz I made famous the expression blinded by the light
Made it rhyme with night
Made them extreme opposites
And then put them right next to each other
Like Siamese Twins
Cuz I'm the one you can hide your guilt within
Blend in
Or
Submerge

I'm the impulsive Urge
I come without words
I'm the Crack vile on the playground curb
I'm that absurd
I beat your wife in the suburbs
I'm the quick fist
I'm the Nucleus
The Solar Eclipse while the North Star drips
The perverted Elf in the darkness
That Hollywood, Colt 45, bare chest action, that no
person can harness
You can categorize and name this
But never tarnish
Cuz to brand this is outlandish
And Ultimately Self-Defeating
I'm his Bobby Digital Existence
Drunk, Slim, and shady
Body heat seekin camouflaged under breath mints
I gave you the negative alphabet syndrome
I'm Full Blown
I'm the paranoid insecurity when you get stoned
I'm your hatred of skin tones
I'm the depression at night when you feel alone
The impatient frustration when your luxury service
signals roam
Your mental Cyclone

And sadly, I'll finally rest, only cuz I'm tired of walking
And eventually, you'll still walk in
The sickness of my hipness
I'm the opposite of a family doctor

You Come to me for disease
Priceless and Worthless
Take a picture, It won't develop
Worse, you can never escape the negative
Cuz I was Cain when you thought you were able
I swept your feet when you thought you were stable
I'm the final straw
The 2 of clubs on the final draw
So Come Close
For me to eject through these mediums of journey
Someone has earned me
Quietly yearned me
I'm sitting with you
I permeate and procreate in the lies of truth
The fallacies of laws are the biggest clue
This is only a written spew
From the cuckoo nest over which I flew
I'm in morning dew
You think it's early – I been waitin for you
I'm premeditated and postmarked
I'm the referee
You can't cheat me
I'm the foul you call
The Long Hall
The one you pass slowly by
You know why
N' the only way to Reject me
Is to listen and accept me
Like an allergy, there'z no cold turkey
First, believe in We

I filled the gaps of your destitute energy
I'm the idleness in idolatry
You cradle me, Naturally
Stop mocking me
Only your secrecy can deplore me
Abhore and ignore me
But I'm not a choice like the red devil on your shoulder
I'm the boulder
Pounding into your head like migraines
That's my pain
I'm always in Vain
I'm the one you were talking to when you should have
been walking to
Another destination
I'm patient
N look at you, surface tiled
Rolling your eyes, tweakin
Never disregard the voicebox speakin
He's washin clean while your conditioned behaviors
are leakin
Pass your insecurities and call him crazy
Hypocrites never cease to amaze me
Just keepin passin the courvoisier baby
All those emotions to uncover and I scared you into lazy
Parasitic style plagues me
Thus I continue to persist through child and adult times
With health I wait to cut the life line
I jump hosts and slowly watch you unwind

That same dirty animal in the back of your mind
The one who comes out in poetry givin a Fuck If
I ever rhyme

THE WILLOW

July 23, 2011

A giant
A dinosaur of her species
I love the nature of these trees
The matriarchal mother
Supportive and longing to hold you in her arms

Rooted in character
Loyalty and perseverance
She is resilient to the forces of all seasons
Respect earned quietly
Her actions speak louder than words
She is not clumsy or uncoordinated but rather graceful
Swaying to and fro
She is a symbol of family
Always present
And still willing to grow

Ben, Tom and Dylan under
the willow where Max's
ashes are buried.

"I always thought we'd
have more time."
— Cousin Dylan Miller Evans

Thoughtful Max.

THE MAIN QUESTION IS WHY?

Why would an attractive, creative young man end up dead from an overdose at an age when he would normally be enjoying the successes of his gifts? The simple answer to this painful question is because Max Monroy-Miller was an addict. Max was one of those unfortunate individuals who inherited a genetic disposition to addiction, along with many in our communities. That reality combined with various aspects of his life story, meant that at some time prior to his death his use of alcohol and drugs triggered a neurochemical reaction that resulted in him being certain that this was the greatest thing he had ever experienced. Max was home.

To recreate this reaction would require an ever-increasing use of drugs and alcohol. The only way he could control this response would be to dedicate himself to an alcohol and drug free lifestyle. Max never fully accepted this reality.

Addiction in all of its ramifications is a deadly disease for anyone. This effects people from all socio-economic levels of our society. Addiction is an equal opportunity killer. This reality has been playing out in too many of our communities for decades. While this horrible reality is on the rise, success with recovery is also possible for many. Why then was young, bright, creative Max Monroy-Miller not one of those to rise from the depths of addiction? The answer to that question is as complex and obscure as any in the realm of human behavior.

After a life in addiction and addiction recovery the best I can offer is that recovery requires acceptance of total powerlessness to control drug use. Once an addict starts, he can't stop.

The mind wants to believe it will be different this time. The mind seeks that magical high again.

The mind fights acceptance of that reality until some event creates a crisis so significant that the individual's view of reality changes. I have called that event soul-cracking.

In the recovery community it has long been observed that individuals who have achieved higher levels of worldly success often have a very difficult time accepting that very powerlessness that is at the core of recovery. This happens whether the successes come in the form of large amounts of money, academic degrees, or job promotions, or in the willingness of colleagues and loved ones to be accepting and encouraging of the failures along the way. The addict will use anything and everything to rationalize away their addiction. The fact is that to use is to engage in a suicidal act that will eventually and inevitably end in death.

Individuals do not ever go into the world to become addicted. They go into the world to enjoy life and prosper. When addiction occurs the addict either experiences the soulcracking and responds by accepting help, or they die of the disease. For loved ones it is fundamental to accept they cannot make it happen for the addict.

They can pray and beg but, in the end, only the addict can make the decision to accept the terrifying reality that this behavior which feels like it is the only thing that can make them happy is the very thing that will end their life.

Joseph B. Kelly, MA, LPC, CAC

Minister of Friends of the Light
Max's spiritual home

Drawing of his character Mr. Love, by Max Monroy-Miller

SHOOTING STAR

His burned fast, rocketed high, got high, dimmed early.

"Max is dead." An irrevocable thud in three words.

I fell onto my green couch. How could my sisters be on the phone with these words?

A muted crash many could see coming.

Typing his poems of ten years ago, his words now strike such prescient tones. Gone over four years, ahead of his time. He seemed to know his parking meter was expiring.

Even pensive, contemplative, inert photos of him belie a wild whirling of his electrons.

He walked at nine months and ran hard the rest of his thirty-eight years.

He performed when entering a room and we provided the stage, our ticket to the Max show. A student artist in San Miguel, a photographer with a gallery show on Valencia Street, a fraternity founder, an MSU Chicano Studies Department advocate, a spoken word performer, a poet, a state football championship tight end, a homeowner, a high school VP, ahead of his times, killed by his times.

He flew through new projects, countries, languages, communities, attracting friends and colleagues – many believing they were his best friend. In a hurry to bring his gifts. He made you laugh at yourself because he nailed your foibles in a tease – and you could let him, because you felt the love, the honesty.

His Achilles heel, he repeatedly remortgaged the deed to defeat his addiction that became a top killer in 2016. That deed, only purchased with total admission of complete defeat. Nobody conquers it alone. Ever.

The addiction was always stronger, scrambling his frontal lobes as crack does. His car turned left to the dealer instead of right to his fiancé. Impossible to control the wheel. At his memorial, his PhD cohort barely aware of his peril, instead dazzled by his once bright star. Even super-human willpower could not quite hide his sweating and shaking hands. But after years, we who knew him best, saw his bright star dimming.

We sent him off in style from the gazebo in Old Settler's Park that rainy June day. The gray skies opening with just enough sunshine for loving speeches, dispersing his poems, photos, spoken word and political rants, and now publishing a book, in hopes that maybe, just maybe, one haunted being will turn their car the other way. Just maybe his story could alter the strangling, soul-disfiguring pull of addiction. That would be the true revolution.

Our man was very well loved, so publicly paid attention to, but his suffering ran long and deep, abetted by the numbing, chiseling away of his gifts, his hopes. Our hopes now — that some of his gifts are preserved... in this little book. We continue to speak your name, dear Max.

Your loving Aunt Jannie who gets it,

Janet Miller
October 2020

"Mr Love" cake for Max's Memorial, June 2016; created by his Aunt Nancy, Max's art mentor and travel companion.

ICARUS FALLING

Jean Golden, March 15, 2017
On the one-year anniversary of Max's death

You dreamed you could
Soar higher
than any other
That the laws
Of gravity
Did not apply
To you.

I watched
As you carefully
Constructed
Your wings
Of wax, and feathers.
Believing,
As all believers
do, that your
Path would lead
To the heavens.

I listened, as you
Convinced
Your faithful
Followers that you
Could do
What no one
Else had done.

That wax
And feathers
Would hold your
Fragile body
As you lifted,
Like Icarus
Into the clear
Blue sky,
Alone.
I watched as you
Floated higher,
The rippling waves
Of heat
Making you giddy
As the air
Grew thin, and
The oxygen rare.

Watched, as your
Wings began
To melt
And you fell,
Unconscious
Back to the earth,
Twisting slowly,
Already sleeping
The sleep
Of no dreams.

Leaving us,
Your followers,
To mourn,
And question,
Question our faith
In wings,
And heaven.
To question
Our faith
In dreams,
And in ourselves

San Miguel de Allende, 2005

ACKNOWLEDGEMENTS

Thank you to Dan Stewart, who crossed my path at random and in hearing about Max's story encouraged me to find a way to publish his work so that others could benefit; to Melissa Fournier, who has given me loving support and encouragement for my own writing and for sharing Max's work; and to Holly Wren Spaulding, an old family friend who guided me in organizing these poems into a package to share. These people are teachers with heart. I am forever grateful.

My dear friend Jacob Wheeler referred me to Mission Point Press. Doug Weaver and Angela Saxon are helping to create a very special collection of Max's work. Lisa Newhouse has offered me such valuable assistance with the necessary technology. I would be at a loss without this support.

My precious family and friends have offered support along the way. This has kept me going. My sisters Janet and Nancy Miller have given me just what I needed, each in their own way. My lifelong friends Ellin Woods and Arthur Melnick also supported my efforts each in their own way.

And mostly, I am grateful for my talented son Max, who lived his life to the fullest and left me so much beautiful work to share. He will be remembered and cherished forever.